Contents

		Page
1	In the Beginning	1
2	George Ramsay	3
3	The Ground	5
4	Early Days	7
5	1895	9
6	Down So Long	11
7	Deadly Doug	12
8	Brian Little	15
9	Europe	19
10	Dwight Yorke	22
11	Savo Milosevic	24
12	Stan Collymore	26

The 1997 Aston Villa Squad.

1 In the Beginning

There's only one team
in the West Midlands.
And that's the Villa.

Forget Birmingham City –
with them you just get the Blues.
Forget West Brom.
Forget Coventry and Walsall Town.

We've won the FA Cup seven times and
we've won the League Cup seven times.
We've won the League four times,
and the European Cup once – in 1982.

So forget the rest.
There's only one Aston Villa.

Aston Villa was one of
the first football clubs in England.
We began life in 1874.

Near Aston, in Birmingham,
there was a chapel.
It was called
the Villa Cross (Aston) Chapel.

The young men of the chapel
played cricket.
But they also wanted something to do
in the winter.
They wanted to play football.

So they put a team together.
There was a big house
on a corner near the chapel.
It was called Aston Villa.
That was how the team got its name.

Villa's first match was in March 1874.
That long ago,
there were not that many teams
in Birmingham.

So the Villa played a local rugby team.
It was called
Aston Brook St Mary's Rugby Team.
Both teams had 15 a side.

In the first half, they played rugby.
At half time, the score was still 0–0.

In the second half,
they played football instead!
With 15 men, Villa had 7 strikers!
And they won 1–0.
Of course!

2 George Ramsay

George Ramsay
was the Villa's captain.
He really put the new club
on the map.

He came from Glasgow
in 1876.

He saw the Villa players
kicking a ball about
on Aston Park,
and near the Villa Park
that we know today.

George asked the others:
'Can I join in?'

The Villa players weren't sure at first.
The new player
was small and skinny.

But in the end,
they gave him a game.

George Ramsay stayed with the Villa
for the next 59 years.
George Ramsay was captain,
then secretary,
then Vice President of the club.

In that time,
he saw Villa
win their first trophy:
the Birmingham Senior Cup
in 1880.

They went on to win
the FA Cup six times,
and the League six times.

And all that
before Ramsay retired
in 1935!

3 The Ground

To begin with,
the Villa played in open fields.
They were the Aston Lower Grounds,
near Aston Hall.

Then, in 1876, they moved
to a proper ground at Perry Barr.

At the time, their nick-name
was the Perry Barr Pets!

At first, women did not have to pay
to go to watch the Villa play.
Then, after 1886, they paid half price.

The Villa stayed at Perry Barr
for 20 years.

1896–97 was a big year
for Aston Villa.
We won the double.
And we moved to Villa Park.
We are still there to this day.

Villa Park.

4 Early Days

There are some strange stories
from Villa's early days.

One early Villa player
always wore a woolly hat
when he played!

In one match,
there was heavy rain.
One player played the match
holding an umbrella
over his head!

In November 1898,
Villa played Sheffield Wednesday.
After 80 minutes,
the game was stopped.
The last ten minutes
were played later –
four months later, in March 1899!

Villa lost,
so the rest did not do them any good!

In one Cup match in 1883,
Villa were losing 4–3.
A Villa shot was heading for goal
to make it 4–4.
But a defender punched the ball
off the line.

Villa complained to the ref.
But there were no penalty kick laws
in those days.
Villa got a free kick,
but they didn't score from it.
So the score stayed at 4–3,
and Villa went out of the Cup!

Eight years later, in 1891,
Villa were playing Stoke.
We were winning 2–1.
But in the last minute,
Villa gave away a penalty.

A Villa player kicked the ball
out of the ground.
And a Stoke player had to go
and fetch it back for the penalty.

But the ref blew the final whistle
before the Stoke player got back!
The law was changed
at the end of that season.

5 1895

But the strangest Cup stories
come from 1895.

Villa beat West Brom 1–0,
in the FA Cup Final.
John Devey, the Villa captain
got into the record books.
His winning goal
came in the first 30 seconds.
It was the fastest ever goal
in an FA Cup Final.

(Villa's goal in 1895
beat Chelsea's 1997 goal,
scored by Roberto di Matteo,
by 13 whole seconds!)

Back in 1895,
the proud Villa team
took the Cup back to Birmingham.

It was put on show
in the window of a Birmingham shop.
But it wasn't there for long.

On the night of 11 September 1895,
somebody broke into the shop.
The Cup, and some money, were taken.
Luckily, Villa had insured the Cup for £200.
The police offered only a £10 reward.
Perhaps that was why
the FA Cup was never found.

Villa won the FA Cup again,
two years later.
Another one had had to be made!
This time Villa took more care of it!

63 years later, somebody confessed.
In 1958, aged 83,
a man called Harry Burge
said he'd taken the Cup
all those years ago.
Harry was a local man.
He was well-known to the police.
He had spent nearly 50 years
of his life in prison.

Harry said that
he and his friends melted it down,
and made it into coins.
He said that he spent the money.
Some of it was spent on beer
in a pub owned by a Villa player!
Not everyone believed Harry's story.

6 Down So Long

The club's low point
came in the late 1960s.
In the last game of 1966–67,
we lost 6–2 to Southampton.
We had only got two points
from the last 16 matches.
Second Division here we come!

Next season we finished 16th
in Division Two.
Both on the pitch and off the pitch,
Villa were in a bad way.
We were short of money
and short of good players.

In spite of our problems,
we still got to Wembley.
We were runners-up
in two League Cup Finals.
One in 1968, one in 1970.
But by then we'd sunk
to the Third Division!

7 Deadly Doug

One man saved Aston Villa
from disaster.
Doug Ellis was a local business man.
He ran a travel agency.
Doug Ellis became Chairman
of Aston Villa Football Club.
He ran the business.
He re-built Villa Park
and sorted out the money problems.
He brought the club
into the modern age.

Doug Ellis is still in charge
at Villa Park.
He has seen times change.
He has seen a lot of players
come and go.
A lot of managers too.
But he knows what's best for the club.

Once,
somebody called him 'Dirty Doug'.
He wasn't happy.
'No, you're wrong there,' he said.
'The name's "Deadly Doug"!'

Doug Ellis, the Aston Villa chairman.

In football nowadays,
managers often get the sack.
Doug Ellis started the trend
of sacking managers.

He has sacked seven Villa managers.
One manager told the press:
'The Chairman has said
he's right behind me.
But I told him –
I prefer him in front of me.
So I can see what he is up to!'
A week later,
that manager was sacked!

In 1971, the tide turned for Villa.
Villa won promotion
from Division Three.
We got 70 points – another record.
And the Villa Youth Team
won the FA Youth Cup.

Villa had been building a youth team
for a number of years.
They were the players of the future.
And they were already showing
they knew how to win!

One of the 'players of the future'
was a young man called Brian Little.

8 Brian Little

Brian played for Villa for 11 years.
He was a midfield genius.
In nearly 300 matches,
he scored 82 goals.

He saw the Villa side go up
from Division Three
to the very top of Division One.

And he helped Villa
win the League Cup Final in 1977.
Villa beat Everton 3–2.
Little scored two goals.

Brian stopped playing
because of a knee injury.
But he couldn't bring himself
to leave Villa.
He ran the Youth Team.

Later,
he became manager of Leicester City.
Under Brian,
Leicester went up into the Premier League.

Brian Little the midfield genius!

But he said:
'I love it at Villa.
I'd go back tomorrow ...'.

In November 1994,
Villa manager Ron Atkinson
was sacked by Doug Ellis.

It was quite a shock to Big Ron.
'In the morning,' he said,
'I was shopping for Stan Collymore.
By the afternoon,
I was in Sainsbury's,
shopping for cauliflower!'

Brian Little told the press
he had no plans to leave Leicester.
But two days later,
that's just what he did.

And so the Villa hero came back to Aston Villa.
Leicester were not happy.
Little had broken his contract.
Villa had to pay huge fines.

One of Villa's next games
was against – guess who?

The Leicester fans felt let down.
They really let Brian know
just what they felt about him.

The match ended 1–1,
so there were no winners
and no losers that day.

Brian Little led Villa to victory
in the Coca Cola Cup in 1996.
They won 3–0 against Leeds.

Just like Ron Atkinson had done
two years earlier.
Then, the Villa had won 3–1
against Manchester United.

But Leicester then went on
to win the Coca Cola Cup in 1997.

9 Europe

Winning the Coca Cola Cup
means a ticket to Europe.
But all in all,
Villa have not done so well
in Europe.
Often they have gone out
in the first few rounds.
But in 1981–82, they went all the way.

Villa got to the European Cup Final.
They played the German giants
Bayern Munich.
Villa beat them 1–0.

Then, in January the next year,
Villa played Spanish champions
Barcelona.
This was in the European Super-Cup.
In Barcelona, Villa lost 1–0.
But we thrashed them 3–0
back at Villa Park.

The 1982 European Cup Winners – Aston Villa!

Villa beat the best teams in Europe,
and made it look easy!

Villa fans will be hoping
for more Cup wins –
both at home and in Europe.

And slowly but surely,
Villa are building a winning team.

A lot depends on our three main strikers:
Dwight Yorke, Savo Milosevic
and Stan Collymore.

10 Dwight Yorke

Dwight went to school in Trinidad,
with two famous sports stars.
One was West Indies cricket star
Brian Lara.
The other was Newcastle goal keeper
Shaka Hislop.

Dwight was Villa's top scorer
in 1996–97.
But he will have to be good
to beat Villa's other two goal scorers.

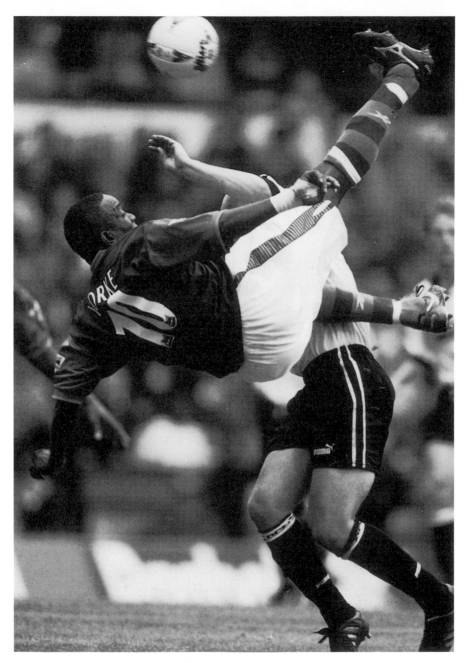

Dwight Yorke scores again.

11 Savo Milosevic

Savo is Serbian, born in Bosnia.

Brian Little decided to buy Savo
from Partisan Belgrade.
Why spend over £3 million?
Because Savo had just scored 75 goals
in one season!

Savo can't always get a place
in the Villa first team.
But Dwight Yorke gets more goals
when Savo plays.

And Savo can score one or two himself.
Remember that rocket shot
he scored in the 1996 Coca Cola Cup Final?

Savo Milosevic scoring in the 1996 Coca Cola Cup final.

12 Stan Collymore

Stan Collymore wanted
to move from Liverpool.

He was born near Birmingham.
And he's always been a Villa fan.

Brian Little had wanted
to sign Stan for quite a while.
In the end, Stan came to Villa
for £7 million (a club record).
That was in the summer of 1997.

Stan can be a bit head-strong.
A bit big-headed even.
In the past,
he fell out with team mates.
He fell out with his managers.

But he kept on scoring goals.
And now, when he's not scoring goals,
he's making goals for team mates,
like Robbie Fowler at Liverpool.
That's a new side to Stan's game.
One that Dwight and Savo
were looking forward to!

Stan Collymore.

1997 was an important year
in the history of Aston Villa Football Club.

It was 100 years
since the move to Villa Park
in 1897.

That same year, 1897,
Villa won the League,
and won the FA Cup too.
Villa's last FA Cup win
was in 1957.
Brian Little was three years old at the time!

So maybe it's time
the Villa won the FA Cup again.

But remember:
one FA Cup has been stolen
from Villa.

When we win it *next* time,
we'll make sure
nobody takes it off us!